For Liam and Max,
Edie and Leo,
Cliona, Alana and Deanna.

Also available from Ruwanga Trading,
**   dba HawaiianChildrensBooks:**

The Goodnight Gecko
The Brave Little Turtle
The Magical Journey from Hawaii
Hoku the Seal's Three Wishes
The Rainbow Mermaids of Hawaii
Happy as a Dolphin, a Child's Celebration of Hawaii
The Whale Who Wanted to be Small
The Gift of Aloha
The Shark Who Learned a Lesson
Gecko Hide and Seek
Tikki Turtle's Quest
How the Geckos Learned to Chirp

For more information and gift set ideas, visit Gill's website:
www.HawaiianChildrensBooks.com/collections/gift-sets

Follow Us on **Instagram** - @hawaiianchildrensbooks

Find Us on **FaceBook**: Gill McBarnet - HawaiianChildrensBooks.com

First published 2021 by Ruwanga Trading
ISBN 978-0-9701528-8-6
Printed in China by Everbest Printing Co., Ltd

BOOK ENQUIRIES AND ORDERS:

aloha@hawaiianchildrensbooks.com

Grateful thanks (mahalo) to Hōkūao and Kanani (Kamehameha School-Maui),
for checking correct usage and spelling of Hawaiian words (hua' ōlelo Hawai'i)

Our Island Home

Counting our Blessings in Hawai'i

by Gill McBarnet

Bless this house our island home,
and our yard with all that's grown.

Long ago, homes (hale) in Hawai'i were made of thatched pili grass and were mainly located on the breezy coastline or as close as possible to rivers for fresh

2 cats • **1** dog (*ī'īlio*) • **1** mountain (*mauka*) • **1** ocean (*makai*) • **1** house (*hale*) • **1** beach (*kahakai*) • **2** buckets

water (wai) for drinking, as well as farming.

• **15** red ʻōhiʻa lehua flowers • **4** Hawaiian geese (*nēnē*) • **2** Scarlet Honeycreeper (*iʻiwe*) • **14** ʻōhiʻa lehua trees

Bless the places where we roam, from misty forests...

Legend: *Pele the volcano goddess fell in love with Ōhiʻa the handsome warrior, but he loved Lehua. This angered Pele so she turned Ōhiʻa into a twisted tree.*

The other gods were saddened by Lehua's tears so they turned her into the red flower that adorns the ̄ohi'a tree. Now Ōhi'a and Lehua are together, forever.

...to waves that foam.

Kanaloa *was revered as a god of the ocean and long distance voyaging, often represented in the form of a squid or octopus.*

• **1** hermit crab • **1** octopus (*heʻe*) • **3** sea horses • **1** Hawaiian monk seal (*ilioholoikauaua*) • **1** unicorn fish (*kala*) • **1** reef trigger fish (*humuhumunukunukuā-puaʻa*) •

5 anemones • **3** Moorish idol (*kihikihi*) • **4** yellow tang (*lauʻipala*) • **2** parrot fish (*uhu*) • **1** lion fish **1** sword fish

1 hammerhead shark • **1** lobster (*wa*) • **1** starfish • **1** humpback whale (*koholā*) • **3** moon jellies • **1** clown fish • **2** Black Tip reef shark (*mano paʻele*)

Bless the places where we toil, from ocean harvest...

Long ago, *whole communities sometimes used giant nets over 100 feet long for a* **hukilau**. *During hukilau, fish were driven to shallow water by beating the*

water with the leaves (lau) of the ti (ki) plant. People by the shore caught the fish in the net, and the harvest was shared by all who toiled together!

...to rich red soil.

• 14 mangos • 1 shovel • 5 buckets • 8 tomatoes • 4 red ginger flowers • 3 hats • 7 bananas • 2 sunflowers • 5 lemons

In early Hawai'i, a farmer (*mahi'ai*) *grew a variety of crops, and worshipped Lono, the god of agriculture. Crops included taro* (*kalo*), *banana* (*mai'a*),

• **21** cabbages • **1** wheelbarrow • **14** mango leaves • **1** "thank you" (*mahalo*) sign • **6** glasses of juice •

1 juice jug • **13** red ti (*ki*) leaves • **2** chairs • **2** farmers

coconut palms (niu), sweet potato (uala) and breadfruit (ulu).

Bless the places where we play...

Long ago, *the annual "Makahiki" festival was held*

sports like surfing (he'e nalu) were encouraged. Surfing originated in Hawai'i.

in honor of Lono and the nobility (ali'i), and during this time war was forbidden. Makahiki was held from about mid October to mid February, and recreational

... and our music, with hula sway.

• 5 Ti (*ki*) leaf hula skirts • 2 ukulele players • 4 drums • 4 fernhead lei (*haku*) • 2 percussion sticks (*hula puʻili*)

Early Hula was a dance chant accompanied by shark skin drums, nose flutes, gourds and rattles. ***Modern hula*** is often accompanied by stringed instruments

1 conch • **2** black seed lei (*kukui*) • **6** flower lei • **4** hula dancers • **1** Hawaiian nose flute (*ohe hanu ihu*) • **2** ukuleles • **2** feather gourd rattles (*ipu*)

...like the guitar and the 'ukulele. Every year the hula is celebrated at the "Merrie Monarch Festival" in Hilo, Hawai'i.

Bless our schools and all our tools...

"Hālau" is the Hawaiian name for school or academy, and it literally means "A branch from which many leaves grow." The name for a modern school is "kula",

• 1 goalie • 1 goal • 1 shady tree   7 hats • 6 spectators • 9 soccer balls

• 9 soccer players • 1 referee • 1 whistle • 9 water bottles • 1 bleacher

…and our sports, with all the rules.

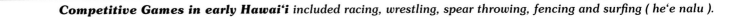

Competitive Games in early Hawai'i *included racing, wrestling, spear throwing, fencing and surfing (he'e nalu).*

Bless the places where we eat,
and our ohana who we greet.

Baby lu'au: In early Hawai'i a huge feast or "aha'aina" was held in honor of the baby. The traditional feast still celebrated by extended family ('ohana),

7 lei • **15** balloons • **1** birthday cake • **2** babies • **2** "Aloha" shirts • **1** candle • **1** rice paddle • **2** food platters • **1** boy (*keiki kāne*) • **3** girls (*kaikamāhine*) •

3 mothers (*mākuahine*) • **1** father (*makuakāne*) • **2** grandparents/elders (*kūpuna*)

includes a pig (pua'a) roasted in a fire pit (imu), seafood, coconuts, sweet potato and "poi" (cooked and crushed root of the taro plant, thinned with water).

**Bless our history, very grand ...
and the mystery of our land.**

1 Erupting volcano – the Hawaiians revered Pele the volcano goddess

• 1 basket weaver

1 Cape, intricately made from bird feathers and worn by the nobility (*ali'i*) • 1 feathered helmet, as worn by King Kamehameha 1, the warrior king who unified the islands

3 Double-hulled Canoes • **10** taro (*kalo*) leaves • **2** baskets made from the leaves of the *"pūhala"* tree • **1** *"lauhala"* mat

between 1790 - 1810 • **1** Royal necklace (*niho palaoa*) • **1** kalo farmer with digging tool (*o'o*) • **4** coconut trees – (*niu*) for food, and to make coconut-fiber rope

Across the islands, every day
we count our blessings
in many ways.

Hawaiian cowboy, "paniolo". There were paniolo in Hawaiʻi in the 1830's, before there were cowboys in the mainland US. They were named after the skilled Mexican cowboys ("Espaniola"- Hawaiians didn't pronounce the "s") who Kamehameha III brought to Hawaiʻi, to teach Hawaiians how to handle large herds of cattle. Large cattle ranches still exist today, like the 130,000 acre Parker Ranch on the Big Island.

Pineapple. Over 150 years ago, climate and rich soil were found to be perfect for pineapples and sugar cane, but global competition has made Hawaiʻi diversify into other crops like coffee, vegetables, fruit and flowers. While Hawaiʻi's main industry is Tourism, there are great efforts to revitalize Hawaiian as well as diversified agriculture again.

Hula dancer. Modern hula is usually accompanied by guitar and ʻukulele, as well as drums and gourds. Leading up to "May Day" every year, children in Hawaiʻi practice Hawaiian songs or chants, and perform hula for their families. From Preschool through to the 12th Grade, May Day is a wonderful celebration of hula.

The ʻukulele ("jumping flea" in Hawaiian) was introduced to Hawaiʻi in 1878. Adapted from a Portuguese string instrument and played by many famous Hawaiian singers, the ʻukulele is now popular across the world.

Humpback whales (*koholā*) spend their winters in Hawaiʻi. From about November to March they give birth to their babies in the tropical water surrounding the islands, where they are protected and admired by visitors and residents. Whale watching boats go out to observe the gentle giants from a respectful distance, and from about April they leave Hawaiʻi and begin their 3,000 mile migration back to their feeding grounds in Alaska.

Coral reefs are 'home' to thousands of species of fish, crustaceans, molluscs, mammals and plant life.